5/15/91

To NICK

EIGHT KISSES ON YOUR BIRTHDAY (YUCK)

GRANPOP.

WILDLIFE OF AMERICA

WILDLIFE OF AMERICA

TEXT BY BILL IVY

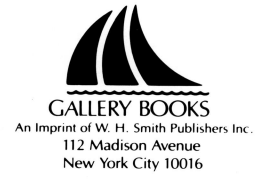

GALLERY BOOKS
An Imprint of W. H. Smith Publishers Inc.
112 Madison Avenue
New York City 10016

Copyright © 1986 Discovery Books

Produced by Discovery Books for:
Gallery Books
An imprint of W.H. Smith Publishers Inc.
112 Madison Avenue
New York, New York 10016

Designed by Marie Bartholomew

Printed and bound in Italy

ISBN 0-8317-9431-3

Pages 2 and 3: When threatened, muskoxen
will form a defensive circle around the cows
and calves.

Page 4: Porcupines are usually found in or near
trees, which supply their favorite food — twigs
and leaves in summer and bark in winter.

Page 8: A cunning hunter, the timber wolf
will often attack animals larger and swifter
than it is.

Table of Contents

Introduction

Wilderness — how does one begin to define it? To some, it is symbolized by the eerie call of a loon echoing across a misty lake or the lonely bellow of a cow moose breaking the stillness of a drowned land. In others, it evokes the image of a pack of wolves crossing a moonlit ice field or of an eagle soaring effortlessly above an alpine meadow. Yet to many the wilderness is synonymous with loneliness, monotony and fear: the ominous silence and remoteness are too great a challenge.

North America's wilderness is all this and more. It is miles and miles of untamed land, vast tracts of relatively undisturbed forests, mountains, deserts, plains and tundra. Every type of environment with the exception of tropical forest and grasslands is represented here. Each habitat supports its own unique community of flora and fauna. From the frozen Arctic to the humid mangrove swamps, each of these areas harbors an incredible variety of wildlife.

North America is home to more than 400 land mammals, over 650 species of birds and upwards of 500 different reptiles and amphibians, not to mention more than 150,000 species of insects! It is a land of contrasts and its wildlife reflects this fact. This continent's mammals range in size from the three-and-a-half-inch pygmy shrew to the ninety-foot blue whale. The pronghorn antelope, beaver, black bear and bobcat are just a few of the mammals that can be found only in North America. Its bird life is just as diverse. For example, the tiny three-and-a-half-inch ruby-throated hummingbird is dwarfed by the giant California condor with its enormous ten-foot wingspan. Many varieties of birds are unique to North America: the cardinal, blue jay, bald eagle and black-capped chickadee are just a few.

Early European settlers on this continent found a land teeming with wildlife. In their shortsightedness they hunted and trapped to near extinction many of our grandest mammals, including the bison, pronghorn antelope and muskox. They took for granted the wilderness and wildlife we now prize. Our natural legacy is not an indestructible, inexhaustible resource to be exploited, but rather a treasure to be protected and preserved.

Thanks to the efforts of conservation groups and concerned citizens, laws have been enacted to protect what is wild. Yellowstone National Park, the first national wildlife park in the world, was established in 1872. Other nations soon followed the United States' example. Measures like this have preserved an amazing number of our native wildlife species, and will, we hope, insure their survival for future generations. However, all wildlife must constantly move away from settlements or learn to live in harmony with the ever-increasing encroachment of man.

Distribution Map

North America is the third largest continent. Not surprisingly, geographic and climatic conditions vary dramatically from coast to coast. Nevertheless, each region, no matter how hostile, hosts a tremendous variety of wildlife. Twice annually, millions of birds travel the length of the continent following time-honored flyways, affording even the least adventurous of us an opportunity to view some of North America's most popular species.

Irus

aribou

St. John's

moose

osprey

eaver

Gulf of
St. Lawrence   harbor seal

ec •   •/Halifax

red fox

bobcat   Boston

ce Ontario   •

harbor seal

New York

ington

ATLANTIC OCEAN

ow
ose

ada
e

harbor seal

n
mi
•

The High Arctic

More than a quarter of North America lies in the Arctic Circle. Despite the fact that this region is locked in ice for three-quarters of the year, an impressive selection of wildlife resides in the land of the midnight sun. Thousands of birds migrate here annually to nest.

Year-round residents include the polar bear, muskox, arctic fox, arctic hare and lemming. Braving the frigid waters of the northern seas are the beluga whale, narwhal, walrus and seal.

A gyrfalcon and its young (*previous page*) in their nest overlooking arctic waters. Gyrfalcons live in the Arctic year-round and feed mostly on gulls, waterfowl, ground squirrels and ptarmigans.

The Sabine's gull (*above*) nests in low, wet tundra, near lakes and along coastal areas. It migrates south to British Columbia in winter.

14

The northern fulmar fishes over open ocean, feeding on small
marine animals and carrion. It lays its single egg on a bare ledge.

A true creature of the North, the arctic wolf has a light-colored coat
and stiff hair on its foot pads to protect them from the cold.

Hunted and feared by man, the wolf is an intelligent and social animal. Wolves travel and hunt in packs, covering a large territory.

Ready to flee if necessary, an arctic hare (*left*) checks its surroundings for signs of danger.

The cheery, energetic common redpoll (*above*) nests in the Arctic and winters anywhere from northern Canada to central United States.

The little arctic fox (*right*) will follow polar bears to the most remote islands to feed on discarded seal carcasses. When rodents emerge from hibernation in spring, the fox will become a hunter as well as a scavenger.

Common murres (*left*) nest in immense seacoast colonies. Each female lays a single egg, which is pear-shaped so it will roll in a circle rather than over a ledge.

The small agile surf scoter (*above*), a large black duck with a distinctive bill, spends much of its life at sea, catching food at the surf line.

Superbly adapted to life in the North, the muskox (*left*) has two layers of fur. The soft inner layer, which retains its body heat, is finer and softer than cashmere.

When approached by wolves, muskoxen (*above*) will group together in a defensive circle and attempt to toss the wolves in the air with their horns, then crush them underfoot.

Lemmings (*above*) are common on the wet arctic plains and are preyed on by many larger animals. When the number of lemmings is reduced, many other species suffer.

The largest ground squirrel in North America, the arctic ground squirrel (*right*) hibernates in the winter. It is preyed upon by many species, among them foxes and eagles.

Two polar bears devour a bloody seal carcass. Polar bears also feed on walruses, seabirds and fish.

Polar bears (*above and following pages*) are protected from the cold by their thick fur — so thick water cannot penetrate it — and by their fat, which provides energy and insulation.

Often found at the southern edge of the ice pack, polar bears weigh up to 1,600 pounds but can cross thin ice with ease because their weight is distributed evenly.

Officially designated in Canada as a threatened species, Peary caribou are smaller and lighter-colored than the barren-ground caribou and prefer to travel in smaller groups.

Barren-ground caribou graze in large groups. Herds containing tens of thousands of individuals migrate to the forest south of the tundra for the winter. They return in spring to breed.

Each spring, caribou (*above*) grow new antlers, which harden by early fall. Then the velvet is scraped off, as shown here. They become polished and clean by October and are shed in winter.

This male king eider (*right above*) is in its full breeding plumage. This duck frequents off-shore reefs, rugged seashores and large lakes along the coast.

The yellow-billed loon (*right below*) is often mistaken for the common loon, which has a dark bill. The yellow-billed is found in the central Arctic and the temperate regions.

Harp seals breed on open sea ice, making them easy prey for hunters. The quarry is the newborn pup, whose fur is highly prized.

Once out of the water, harp seals are clumsy, since they cannot bring their hind flippers forward to help propel themselves.

Perhaps alarmed, these walruses (*above*) take to the water in a group. They feed on the ocean floor, eating clams and other invertebrates, which their facial whiskers help them to locate.

Walruses (*right*) spend days at a time huddled closely together on ice floes, rocky promontories and beaches. Hundreds, even thousands, will gather together for warmth and protection.

The white whale is usually found in schools of up to a hundred. It is also called the beluga, which is Russian for "whitish," and the "sea canary," for its musical underwater sounds.

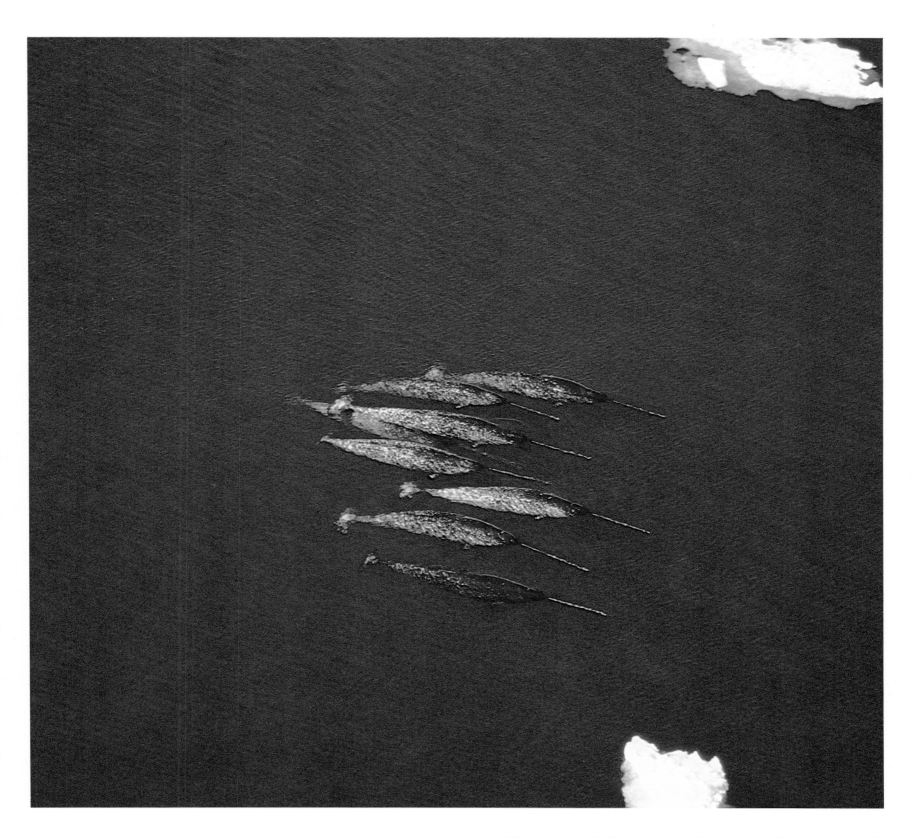

The male narwhal's long twisted horn may indicate social dominance or may be used for defense or feeding. Narwhals, a kind of whale, live in the Arctic year-round, always staying near ice.

Mountains and Valleys

The mountain environment is harsh, and its inhabitants must be hardy and resourceful to survive. Only the sure-footed travel here. Mountain goats and sheep maneuver the rocky cliffs and narrow ledges with apparent ease. During the winter when the climate is severe, most of the animals migrate to the forests, meadows and valleys below. These areas offer a vital sanctuary for the cougar, grizzly, California condor and the golden eagle, all of which are threatened species.

More closely related to antelopes than to the sheep or goats, mountain goats (*previous page*) are agile climbers, scaling sheer rock faces with ease.

A shaggy billy (*above*) surveys his territory.

A mountain goat (*right*) can scramble down a steep cliff.

The majestic bald eagle, symbol of the United States, has declined
drastically in number. Hunting takes its toll, but more harmful is
the presence of pesticides in the eagle's food.

Golden eagles nest on a cliff, their roost lined with sticks and other material. When fully grown, these youngsters will have a wing-span of up to seven feet.

A young bald eagle (*left*) surveys his domain. Bald eagles return to the same nest year after year, adding to the structure until sometimes its weight topples the tree that holds it.

Curious and friendly, the gray jay (*top*) — also called the Canada jay or whiskey jack — frequents camping grounds and logging camps in search of food.

The hoary marmot (*above*) makes its home on the slopes and rockslides high in the mountains.

Larger and less graceful than its eastern cousin the white-tailed deer, the mule deer (*right*) lives in the foothills and mountains of the West. The antlers are shed every spring.

Despite this one's docile appearance, the grizzly bear is considered one of the most ferocious of North America's animals. It gets its name from the grizzled appearance of its fur.

A favorite among big-game hunters, Dall's sheep prefer northerly slopes, particularly in summer when they forage at great altitudes. In winter, they move to lower, southerly inclines.

Wary and solitary, the cougar or mountain lion (*left and above*) is the largest cat and among the most predatory of North America's animals. Its call is a prolonged scream.

Kodiak bears (*above and previous pages*) can weigh two thousand
pounds. They and the polar bear vie for the distinction of being the
largest land carnivore in the world.

Bighorn sheep can scale mountain slopes at up to fifteen miles per hour. The female's horns are thin and spiky; the male's curve in an arc, sometimes forming a full circle.

The red-tailed hawk, seen here in its dark phase, circles high in the air or crouches on lofty perches, looking for rodents and other small mammals.

A pair of Bohemian waxwings feed their young at a nest made of twigs. These birds can catch insects on the wing, but also eat berries and fruit.

Life in the Forest and Field

The forests of North America are as varied as the wildlife they sustain. These coniferous and deciduous woods provide shelter and food for their many inhabitants. In their arboreal homes, owls, hawks and raccoons raise their young. Bear, deer, and grouse roam the forest floor while shrews and mice tunnel beneath. Woodland edges and fields are home to larger burrowing animals such as the badger, skunk and groundhog. These open areas also attract an abundance of birds and butterflies.

The prairie antelope (*previous pages*) or pronghorn is found only in North America. It is extremely fast, averaging speeds of forty miles per hour.

A woodland hunter, Cooper's hawk (*above*) is slightly smaller than a crow and preys on birds and other small animals.

The ruffed grouse is a hardy species found from northern Canada to the central United States.

The eastern bluebird (*left*), the only bluebird with a red breast, frequently nests in woodpecker holes.

Young rose-breasted grosbeaks (*above*) wait for more food, while their mother keeps a watchful eye.

The cape or European hare (*left*) was introduced to North America from Europe — hence its name. It does not make a burrow or den, but hides in dense vegetation for protection.

The eastern cottontail (*top*) produces several litters a year, but few survive. Most fall prey to owls and foxes — or the gun or automobile.

The snowshoe hare (*above*) gets its name from its large hind feet. Its other name, the varying hare, derives from its seasonal color change.

The porcupine (*right*) keeps to itself amid the trees. If disturbed it will erect its spines and arch its back toward its tormentor.

The piliated woodpecker (*above*) prefers forests but has adapted to life in the suburbs. It feeds on beetles and ants as well as berries and nuts.

In winter, white-tailed deer (*right*) will pack down the snow of their favorite feeding ground. The graceful animal is named for its long tail with a white underside.

The skunk (*left*) is a shy creature, but when threatened it defends itself by spraying its attacker with oil from its scent glands.

Aggressive and irritable, the short-tailed shrew (*top*) is one of the few poisonous mammals. It prefers moist forest floors where it can find insects, grubs and snails.

The tiny deer mouse (*above*), found throughout Canada and the northern United States, comes out at night to search for food.

Raccoons (*previous page*) frequently make their den in a hollow tree and generally give birth to three or four young in a litter.

The ruby-throated hummingbird (*above*) beats its tiny wings 3,500 to 4,500 times a minute while hovering, and is capable of flying 500 miles across the Gulf of Mexico during migration.

A blue jay feeds its young in a nest of twigs. Active and aggressive, the jay's bright color and loud cry make it easy to spot. On the ground, it hops rather than walking.

Mourning doves resemble pigeons, to which they are closely related. Both eat nuts, grain and seeds and, unlike other birds, can drink without raising their heads.

The eastern kingbird breeds in Canada and the United States and winters in South America. It waits on a perch until it spies an insect, which it catches on the wing.

Previous pages: About two hundred wild horses live on Sable Island, a wind-swept sandbar off the coast of Nova Scotia.

One of the wildest creatures of the forest, the tree-dwelling marten (*above*) is a savage and efficient killer.

Stalking its prey at night, the lithe lynx hunts alone. Its large, well-furred feet help it to travel on the snow in winter.

Young gray squirrels check to see if the coast is clear before venturing forth. A familiar inhabitant of parks and cities, the gray squirrel does not hibernate in winter.

A young woodchuck peers out of its den. Woodchucks hibernate in winter. According to folklore, if they come out on February 2 and see their shadow, there will be six more weeks of winter.

The shy red fox hunts for rabbits and rodents along the forest's edge, in clearings or on the tundra. Well adapted to a range of climate, the red fox's color can vary from red to black.

The northern flying squirrel is a forest dweller. The fold of loose, furred skin which runs from its wrist to its ankle allows the squirrel to glide from tree trunk to tree trunk. .

A cousin to the wolf, the coyote (*left*) hunts at night, often calling to other members of its pack. This eerie nocturnal sound is part of life on the prairies and foothills.

A bold hunter, the bobcat (*above*) preys on small animals like muskrats, rabbits and birds. It is smaller than the lynx and its ear tufts are not as large, although both cats have short tails.

North America's largest moth, the cecropia (*above*), boasts a wingspan of up to six inches. A member of the giant silk moth family, it lives for just one week in its adult phase.

The tiger swallowtail butterfly (*right*) is one of the most familiar butterflies. Its strong, sailing flight and fondness for garden flowers brings it even into large cities.

The banded purple butterfly lives primarily in open hardwood forests and at forest edges. A strong flier, it sails up and down a glade or road, or may spend much time on a favorite perch.

The painted lady ranges across the continent in areas that are bright and open. It is subject to great periodic fluctuations in abundance, probably caused by parasites or insufficient food supply.

The saw-whet owl gets its name from its call which sounds like the filing or whetting of a saw. A small inquisitive bird, it hunts only at night, preying on little mammals and insects.

Lively and friendly, the American goldfinch has a pleasant song and an unusual swooping flight. It prefers open areas and gardens and feeds on seeds, berries and insects.

Sixty million bison (*left*) once roamed the plains of North America. Now, most of the remaining 35,000 are in national parks. These shaggy beasts travel in herds of four to twenty members.

A solitary, ill-tempered animal, the black bear (*above*) marks its home territory by clawing boundary trees. The smallest North American bear, it is also the most common.

This young black bear is eating an apple. Fully grown, a black bear can weigh 400 pounds and be three feet high at the shoulder.

More sociable than their elders, these black bear cubs play together amidst the trees.

Rivers and Lakes

North America's countless rivers, streams and marshes are home to a vast array of wildlife. In fact, one-quarter of the world's fresh water supply is contained within its boundaries. Beaver, otter, geese, ducks, turtles, frogs and snakes are just a few of the animals that rely on these waterways for their survival.

Snow geese (*previous pages*) migrate from the Arctic, where they breed, to the west coast of the United States, stopping occasionally to feed and rest at marshes and lakes.

An accomplished diver, the oldsquaw (*above*) feeds on shellfish at depths of up to two hundred feet. It is found on both the Atlantic and Pacific coasts and on the Great Lakes.

A brilliantly colored crested wood duck glides among lily pads. It is the only pond duck to make its nest off the ground, usually in a trunk or limb of a tree near the water.

The belted kingfisher (*left*) can dive headfirst into water and catch a fish in its powerful bill. Each bird has its own territory along waterways, and it fishes alone from perches.

For many people, the common loon (*above*), with its ghostly cry, symbolizes the northern lakelands. Loons nest near the water, sometimes on top of muskrat houses.

The muskrat (*above*) builds its home out of mud, sticks and roots. It is the largest North American member of the rat family.

The playful otter (*above right*) is at home on land or in the water. Otters also enjoy sliding down snowbanks and mud banks.

The mallard, with its strikingly handsome appearance, is probably the best-known duck and is the ancestor of domestic ducks.

The leopard frog is another familiar inhabitant of rivers and ponds. It hunts for insects in the short grasses along the shores.

The gray treefrog uses the adhesive pads on its feet to cling to trees, fences and bushes at the edge of woodlands.

The color of the green treefrog, a graceful and elegant creature, can vary from brilliant green to slate gray.

The bullfrog waits for unsuspecting animals to come by. It eats fish, other frogs, ducklings and even its own young.

The spiny softshell turtle is sometimes called the flapjack or pancake turtle because of its unusual, leathery shell.

The painted turtle is fond of soft-bottomed, weedy ponds and marshes. This pretty amphibian is sometimes called the mud turtle.

Blanding's turtle (*left*) spends much of its time in the water, but it does wander about on land or sun itself from time to time.

A pair of stately mute swans (*above*) glide along. These birds feed on plants growing on the bottom of marshes and ponds.

In its spring breeding plumage, a showy golden horn on each side of
its head, the chunky horned grebe is at its most elegant.

Moose enjoy feeding on twigs and shrubs rather than grazing on grasses and lichen as the caribou do.

The cow moose (*left*) lacks the bell of skin and hair that hangs down from the male's throat. The cow gives birth to two young in spring.

Shedding velvet from his antlers, a large bull moose (*above*) browses in the arctic tundra in autumn.

Caught by an unexpected spring blizzard, a Canada goose remains
on the nest despite the snowdrifts forming around it.

Only one day old, this Canada goose gosling will soon be three feet tall and will join its parents on their migration to the eastern U.S.

The distinctively colored great blue heron (*left*) fishes in shallow water for crayfish, frogs and fish. It stands about four feet high.

The great blue heron (*above*) often builds its nest in a dead tree. A platform of sticks, the nest is added to each year.

A northern water snake suns itself on a partly submerged log.
Sometimes mistaken for a water moccasin, the water snake is
harmless, although some of the larger ones can inflict a painful bite.

The spotted salamander lays eggs which hatch into a larval stage with gills, but no legs. Two or three months later, the larvae transform into adult salamanders like this one.

Sea and Shore

The Atlantic and Pacific coasts are constantly changing as the sea battles the shore. Whales and sea otters swim near the shoreline while scores of murres, puffins, gulls and gannets nest on rocky outcrops.

Seals, walruses and sea lions frequent the beaches to rest, breed and bear their young. In the warmer waters of the South, egrets, herons, and pelicans nest in sheltered lagoons.

A flock of pelicans (*previous pages*) with their young nest together. Extremely sociable, pelicans will feed, roost, fly and nest in groups.

The white pelican's long pouched beak is well suited to catching fish, the mainstay of the bird's diet.

Often seen following ships, Thayer's gulls nest in the high Arctic Islands and winter as far south as California.

The bald eagle (*left*) feeds mostly on fish. It catches them near the surface of the water or finds them washed up on beaches. This magnificent bird is most common along the Pacific coast.

The double-crested cormorant (*above*) is another fish-eater. About the size of a goose, it is found along both coasts, where it nests in trees and on the ground. It often perches on wharves and breakwaters.

Harbor seals prefer to hunt alone for squid, fish and molluscs, but
they will gather with others in loosely organized colonies on land.

Harbor seals are one of the most commonly seen seals. They are
found as far south as Baja California and North Carolina.

Thick-billed murres (*left*) nest on rocky cliffs along the coasts. Their wings are used for swimming as well as flying. To get aloft they patter along the water's surface with their webbed feet.

On a cliff above the Atlantic Ocean, a great cormorant (*above*) sits on its nest of seaweed and sticks, watched over by a group of common murres, named after their call, a purring *mur-r-r-e*.

Inquisitive and unsuspicious birds, common puffins (*above*) breed along the Atlantic coast from Greenland to Maine. Like penguins, puffins can seem to "fly" underwater.

A west-coast inhabitant, the tufted puffin (*right*) follows schools of fish at sea and will fill its large bill with as many as forty small fish at a time.

The walrus (*above and right*) is the only marine mammal with two white tusks. Both male and female have tusks, but the female's are shorter. Walruses feed by standing on their heads in water.

A green-backed heron waits stealthily at the water's edge for small fish, crayfish and insects, which it catches in its sharp, pointed bill. When alarmed it will stretch its neck and raise its crest.

Northern gannets (*above*) lay a single egg in a nest of seaweed or other vegetation high on a cliff of an island in the Gulf of St. Lawrence. They winter along the Atlantic coast.

Ospreys (*following pages*) are excellent hunters and are the only hawks that dive underwater. These osprey have returned to their nest, built of sticks high in a tree, with a fish for their young.

Along the rocky isles of the Pacific coast, colonies of northern sea lions (*above*) congregate during the breeding season. The single pup is born on the beach and is nursed for three months.

Like walruses, sea lions can bring their rear flippers forward when walking on land. Unlike walruses, they are not hairless. The male sea lion (*right*) has a mane and can be four times as large as the female.

The aptly named lesser yellowlegs feeds on small fish and aquatic insects along the shores of marshes, mud flats and ponds.

Two whimbrels share a rocky perch with a group of ruddy turnstones, which get their name from their habit of overturning stones in search of food.

The arctic loon nests in the Far North. Like all loons, its legs are set far back, making it difficult for it to walk on land. Loons' nests are therefore always close to the water.

The shell of the enormous Atlantic leatherback turtle is covered with smooth skin instead of large plates. The world's largest turtle, it spends its entire life at sea, except when breeding.

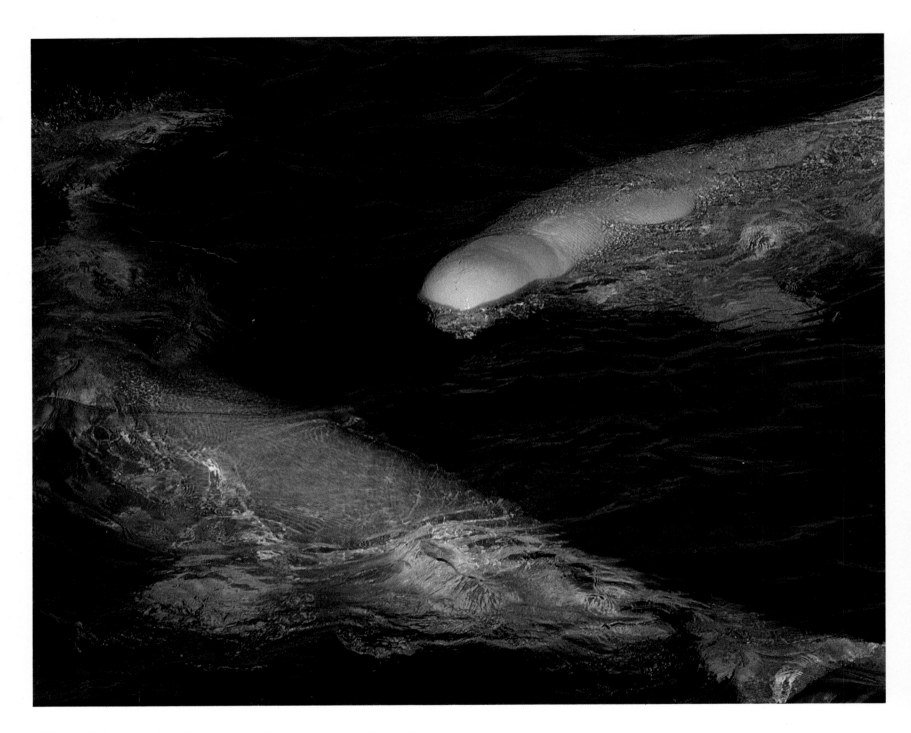

White or beluga whales often join together in large schools numbering hundreds of individuals. The smaller slate-colored calves can be seen (*previous pages*) beside the large white females.

The killer whale (*above*), with its striking black and white markings, is found in all oceans, but mostly in cool water. It preys on fish and seals, but will also attack large whales.

The marbled godwit (*following page*), a large member of the sandpiper family, is usually found in shallow water or marshy shores. It winters in South America.

Photo Credits

Index